Christopher (Christo) Lloyd (aged 17) with his mother Daisy wearing a dirndl costume after her first visit to Austria, his sister Letitia, with their spaniel Bunch, circa 1938.

Many of you will know the multifaceted nature of Great Dixter, either as visitors of a day or after a more prolonged stay in its gardens and nurseries set around the hub of the half-timbered house. So you will be well aware that Christopher Lloyd was born, lived and worked here all his life and made the place what it is today. It was his source of inspiration and creativity in more ways than one. Plants and gardening from the year dot, teaching and writing. Close at heel came his gift for languages and music, being well-versed in French and German as well as a talented pianist and oboist. He had, as a gardener, an innate sense of colour combinations reflected in his embroidery, many examples of which are scattered around the house. He also came to relish cooking latterly and took up his runcible spoon with great art. No nonsense cookery there!

However, none of this would have been possible had he not made copious notes and plans. What he saw in others people's gardens that piqued his interest as he passed by, he would note, before putting pen to paper or trowel to turf. I would not say he kept a gardening diary, but his numerous gardening notebooks that fill several drawers amount to that. What to remember and when to do it.

The perpetual diary by Sarah Charles that follows is here to remind you of your next step, based on your own observations and experience. Gardens are, from the outside, areas of great repose. But you will know all you have put into it to make it so, with your diary as your defence.

Whether your garden is labour-intensive or not, keeping a gardening diary is useful if only to note the dates of the next flower show, or when a plant flowered and how it tied into your planting scheme, when to trim the hedges and even with wild gardening when to cut. You can plan your holidays accordingly. And if you don't take your diary with you, you can leave others a list of instructions in it of things to do in your absence. (It's so nice to know they're thinking of you while you're away!)

There are infinite ways to make good use of a perpetual diary. Nothing in a garden stands still for long, so to memorize achievements and bear in mind things to come, a perpetual diary is just the framework you need. Take out your pens and use this Dixter diary in your own way, with plenty of advice by Christopher Lloyd. Welcome in yet another way to Great Dixter.

Olivia Eller
Art historian and one of Christo's nieces

LECTURES AND SYMPOSIUMS

Great Dixter invites a number of external speakers to lecture on a variety of topics, such as plants and gardening, biodiversity and the history of the house. Go to our What's on page on our web site and filter for 'Lectures and Talks' to see a list of forthcoming events. Subjects include: The Art of Gardening, Great Dixter's Gardening Year, Garden-Worthy Plants, Choosing and Using Seeds, and Nursery Propagation Day.

Symposiums with Fergus are held three times a year – in February, July and November. They are one week in duration and run from Saturday through to the following Saturday. These courses are of both a practical and theoretical nature, are held in the lecture room and the garden, and include trips to other gardens. Other than having the right gear and the necessary travel arrangements in place, attendees are comprehensively looked after by the Great Dixter team. Accommodation, meals, and if required transport to and from the airport are included within the price of the course.

Complimenting our in-house lecture programme, Fergus Garrett, Head Gardener and Chief Executive of the Great Dixter Charitable Trust, visits and speaks at numerous external events during the year. Go to our What's on page to see external events that Fergus is speaking at.

To book Fergus to speak to your group or Horticultural Society, please email Sarah Seymour: sarah@greatdixter.co.uk

SPECIAL EVENTS

In addition to our seasonal openings from Spring to Autumn we also have Special Events. These include: Winter and early Spring openings highlighting snowdrops and other early flowering plants, Wood Weekend in the medieval Great Barn, oast houses and wood workshop, and the Plant Fair and the Christmas Fair.

FRIENDS OF GREAT DIXTER

Be a part of a growing number of like-minded individuals who wish to see Great Dixter secured as a place where people can meet, exchange thoughts and share ideas. The Friends of Great Dixter is for everyone who has a love of plants, gardens and dynamic planting.
For details about the Friends of Great Dixter Membership and to join, please email: friends@greatdixter.co.uk

COURSES AND SCHOLARSHIPS

Great Dixter is now a charitable trust relying on donations, bequests, and income earned by opening the House, Gardens, Nurseries, Gift Shop and Café. Alongside this we are fortunate in being able to offer day courses, welcoming an increasing number of visitors and gardeners wanting to learn gardening the Christopher Lloyd way.

In addition, we offer three live-in scholarships lasting one year to young enthusiastic gardeners. This gives them a chance to 'live the garden', developing skills and becoming part of Dixter's investment in British horticulture.

The gardening advice in this book is taken from Christopher (Christo) Lloyd's writings, available in his book collection.

CHRISTOPHER LLOYD'S BOOK COLLECTION

- Succession Planting for Adventurous Gardeners
- Colour for Adventurous Gardeners
- Christopher Lloyd's Gardening Year
- Christopher Lloyd's Gardener Cook
- Dear Friend & Gardener
- Christopher Lloyd and Beth Chatto.
- Cuttings
- Exotic Gardening
- The Adventurous Gardener
- Foliage Plants
- Dear Christo - Memories of Christopher Lloyd

All titles available from Great Dixter Gift Shop and online from www.greatdixter.co.uk

THE CHRISTOPHER LLOYD BURSARY

The Christopher Lloyd Bursary is funded solely by Great Dixter's annual Plant Fair held in October.

It is a little gem of an event with 20 plants stalls, each representing a different nursery. Specialist plant talks are given throughout the weekend at the ringing of the Dixter Nursery bell.

This is an event not to be missed, with exhibitors including nurserymen and women from Sweden, Holland, France and the UK.

Everyone is asked to give a percentage of their profits as a voluntary contribution to fund a young trainee gardener to travel in the UK and overseas. This both widens their experiences and gives them inspiration from visiting gardens, gardeners and plants in the wild.

Witnessing plants and their association first hand was something that Christopher Lloyd considered important for a gardener.

GREAT DIXTER DIARY

WITH GARDENING ADVICE BY
CHRISTOPHER LLOYD

A MONTH BY MONTH PERPETUAL DAY BOOK

SARAH CHARLES

January

The reality of January, in East Sussex, most often had nothing to do with frost or snow. There are days and days of heavy, overcast weather – Beth Chatto's 'dustbin lid' – that just broods over you and weighs down your spirits. Or there is a seemingly endless succession of gales and driving rain. Now and again, there is a day's interlude, when the wind drops, the sun shines and you can feel it on your back, through your clothes. That is bliss and everyone cheers up. *Christopher Lloyd (CL)*

January

The Lloyd family children by the leadlight windows of the Great Hall (from the left); the eldest son Selwyn followed by Oliver, Patrick, Quentin, Letitia and Christo, the youngest child on the end.

Above: The Great Hall is original to the fifteenth century Hall House, where the family ate their meals every day. Measuring 40ft by 25ft by 31ft high (12.2m by 7.6m by 9.5m), the building is one of largest surviving timber framed halls in the UK.

Right; top, middle and below: The metalwork light, door handle and knocker on the main door, were designed by Lutyens and made by hand especially for the house.

Previous page: The Oast Houses and Great Barn form a perfect backdrop for the Topiary Lawn.

The original front door within the Porch.

New Years Day   1

2

3

4

5

6

7

January

8

9

10

11

12

13

14

Christopher 'Christo' Lloyd with his darling dachshund Dahlia outside the entrance to the Nursery Barn.

'Every garden reflects the individuality of its owner. Gardens are a great giveaway; that in itself makes them fascinating.
The more you observe and take in, one way or another, the more intensely you are living and the younger you will keep in mind, if not in body. Have a good year'.
Christopher 'Christo' Lloyd

A tribute to Christo's love of Dachshunds made of tiles and stones can be found in the Wall Garden, at the north west corner of the House.

Above: A young Christo sitting quietly in the garden knitting. Taught to knit and embroider by his mother Daisy, creating tapestries would also become a pastime he enjoyed.
Left: A cushion embroidered in flame stitch design, made and signed by Christo in 1946.

Above: Christo's childhood perambulator and wheelbarrow.
Left: A young Christo working in the Potting Shed of the Nursery, which he established at Great Dixter in the 1950s, specialising in Clematis and unusual plants.

Christo's Seasonal Gardening Advice

Apart from occasional sorties to sniff the air, January is the month in which to find reasons (book writing is the best of them) for not being, let alone doing things, in the garden, although, of course, winter digging, draining, hedge cutting and other outdoor jobs go on, as the weather permits. The pruning of deciduous shrubs and trees most of all, as this does not depend on the ground being in any particular state; and the fact of the trees/shrubs being naked allows you to appreciate their structure and to decide where and how to thin them so as to improve their shape, let in more light and replace old branches with new. *(CL)*

15

16

17

18

19

20

21

January

22

23

24

25

26

27

28

The Great Hall seen from 'the Squint', a small window in the Solar (the principal private apartment of the medieval house), both in virtually the same state as they were on the completion of restoration in 1911. Right: The Squint Window on the second floor allows a secret peep of the Great Hall.

Christo's Seasonal Gardening Advice

Rose pruning can go on at any time from November to May, but it is one of those jobs I am keenest to get behind me this month. If some readers are shaking their heads over the idea of rose pruning in midwinter, let them leave it till later, especially if theirs is an exposed garden. I have in mind the spring rush that I know will overtake me in March (especially as I have my borders to overhaul then). Better not to have all that on my mind and rose pruning too. *(CL)*

Above: A bunch of Helichrysum, everlasting flowers in front of the windows of the Great Hall.
Below: Upholstered armchair with needle point embroidery worked by Christo's mother Daisy and brother Patrick.

Above: An oil painting of Daisy, Christo's mother, by Mary Wilson, circa 1900, hangs in the Great Hall.
Below: An amusing embroidered cushion worked by Christo, sitting on top of a patchwork quilt which is protecting books in the Parlour. The Parlour was originally used by Daisy for her needlework and later by Christo for his writings, often in his traditional waterproof black notebooks.

29

30

31

February

Increase in day length becomes a headlong rush by the end of this, the shortest month of the year and the last of winter. According to the weather pattern established in January, this is, in temperatures and mood, either a winter month, prolonging the agony, or the beginning of spring. I like February: I like the word and I like the feeling of so much, in my garden, being on the move. (CL)

February

Above: The immaculately trimmed Topiary Peacocks.

Above: The Sunk Garden designed by Christo's father Nathaniel Lloyd.
Right: Plant labels in the Nursery ready to do their job.
Below: The Peacock Topiary Garden set against the perfect backdrop of the House, photographed in the 1920s.

Previous page: The Nursery was started by Christo in 1954. Here he propagated, tended and sold plants for many years.
Inset left: The House as seen from the Nursery looking across the clematis plants.
Inset right: Snowdrops welcome the thought of spring.

1

2

3

4

5

6

7

8

9

Above: Detail of an Edwin Lutyens designed gate.
Right: Dixter's varied bird population includes swallows, cuckoos and nightingales. Some choose to nest in the Porch.

10

11

12

Above: Plants in the Nursery's cold frames including phlox doghouse pink, iris and geranium.
Right: The metal weather vane on the roof of the White Barn.
Below: A word of warning in the Nursery!

13

14

Christo's Seasonal Gardening Advice

The best policy for anyone new to gardening is to do his (your) jobs by the calendar, until he (you) build up sufficient confidence, experience and understanding, to be able to break the rules when it seems sensible to do so. *(CL)*

February

The Upper Moat – Dry, situated between the Terrace, the Topiary Lawn and Hovel. The Upper Moat was drained when the family arrived to form a piece of turf in the shape of a bath. The Hovel is the original 14th century cowshed on the farm and now provides the Exotic Garden with protection from the north west weather.

Snowdrops emerging in the Long Border. The Liliaceae family are well represented, Galanthus Atkinsii being the tallest and largest. With Galanthus Hippolyta nivalis, and common snowdrops running through phloxes.

Christo's Seasonal Gardening Advice

For a blanket of snow to persist all – or even half the month is rare indeed, and it is in February that the snowdrop season reaches its peak. My mother loved to spread snowdrops around into all sorts of odd corners and hedge or shrub bottoms, where you would not, in summer, have thought that there was room for anything, but in winter, when the leaves are off, there is. She would dig up a fast growing clump after it had flowered, pull the bulbs apart, and then carry them in a trug on her arm until she saw a likely spot into which to pop a few. Then on to the next, and the next. *(CL)*

The gardening staff in the 1920s, photographed in front of Lutyens circular steps, with the Benenden Hall house (circa 1500) behind. The Hall was due to be destroyed but was purchased for £75 by Nathaniel Lloyd. Taken apart timber by timber, it was then re-erected on the back of the new Lutyens part of the building.

Above: Winter colour arranged outside the Porch including, Agave americana marginata, Phormiums, and the hardy bromeliad Fascicularia bicolour.
Below: A cosy corner in the Nursery with seed merchants' catalogues and Titch, one of our two estate cats.

15

16

17

18

19

20

21

February

22

23

24

25

26

27

28/29

Above: The entrance to the Nursery, open throughout the year, except from 23 December to 3 January.
Below: The Lutyens designed circular steps leading to the Exotic Garden and Hovel.

Christo's Seasonal Gardening Advice

Rabbits are fond of crocuses, and if I lose most of my blossom and the tips of the leaves, it is because they have entered the garden. In fact it is a good plan to burn up accumulated rubbish on our several heaps, at this stage, otherwise the does will make their stabs (as we call their short breeding holes, in Sussex) in them and there'll be a young generation making the garden its permanent home. (CL)

Above: Nursery greenhouses with our traditional Hawes watering cans.
Right: : Christo's reasons for why we don't label our plants in the garden. "I know this is a bore, when you quickly want a plant's name, sorry'. he writes.

LABELS

The plants at Dixter are unlabelled. I know this is a bore, when you quickly want a plant's name. Generally there is someone to ask. Here are some of the reasons for my not labelling:
1. This is my own, personal garden; I do not have the obligations of an institution like a botanic or National Trust garden.
2. I hate the look of labels. Like a cemetery.
3. They are expensive in terms of both materials and the time needed to list the plants and to write and place the labels.
4. Plants(as against shrubs) need labels that are stuck into the ground. The public removes them, the more easily to read, but does not replace them firmly or even in the right place.
5. It is easier to pop a label into a handbag than try to memorize it on the spot.
6. The wrong label is read for the name of the plant to be identified.
7. Visitors dart into the border, oblivious of footprints, the better to read a label that is out of reach from the front.
8. If all labels are for that reason placed at the front, misapplicatoin of names will be aggravated.
9. Even when plants are clearly labelled, the public will still ask their name if anyone is around to talk to. They're on an outing.
We're trying to work.
Sorry!
Christopher Lloyd

The Upper Moat-Dry below the Terrace, with the Lutyens circular steps. In the distance, the Loggia on the Terrace with the ash trees beyond.

March

There is something sharp and aggressive in the very word. March is prepared to hurl every sort of weather at us. It is the first month of spring but winter still lurks in the wings, ready to return with an ugly leer. Snow is more frequent then in December. Yet it is a jokey sort of snow. As it sits perched on the top of blue grape hyacinths and yellow daffodils, we can scarcely take it seriously and, indeed, it is gone within minutes, until the next squall arrives. Winds are vicious. *(CL)*

March

Top: Head Gardener Fergus Garrett by the 15th century Nursery barn door. The doorway is the entrance to what was the original apple store.
Top right: The entrance to the Nursery is only five foot high so visitors are duly warned to "Duck or Grouse".
Right: Nursery plants enjoy some spring sunhine in the cold frames.
Below: An invitation to make yourself known to Nursery staff.

Previous page: The view across the Orchard to the House.

Christo's Seasonal Gardening Advice

GREAT DIXTER 'BLACK GOLD' COMPOST RECIPE

7 parts loam, 2 parts grit, 2 parts peat, 1 part composted bark.

To make your very own special 'Black Gold' mix, wearing gloves, combine all the ingredients thoroughly. Use a bucket as a measure

For seed sowing:
36 litres of our compost + 115g fertilizer + 20g lime.

For annuals/perennials:
36 litres + 300g fertilizer + 20g lime + 15g Osmocote.

For vegetables/shrubs:
36 litres + 415g fertilizer + 20g lime + 20g Osmocote.

"We never recklessly throw a whole barrowload of compost on to the border and then start forking it in; we would lose track of where the plants are. Instead, we shovel and lay down pockets of compost in between the plants, spreading it out either by hand or with a narrow border fork, tickling it in as we go." *(CL)*

	1
Christopher Lloyd's birthday	2
	3
	4
	5
	6
	7

March

8

9

10

11

12

13

14

Above: The Orchard with the Exotic Garden, Loggia and the House in the background.
Right: The Lower Moat showing Gunnera manicata in the partial shade of the trees. Their leaves are vast, and visitors soon make a track through the long grass to have themselves photographed beneath a leaf.

Christo's Seasonal Gardening Advice

Give me a fine March day with the sound of flies and bees in the air and I'm on top of the world. So are you, but don't let it rush to your head by sowing every packet of seeds in your pile without stopping to think how you'll keep all those seedlings happy when they need more space or when colder weather returns. It's one thing to have a propagator in which you can germinate the seeds of half hardy annuals at the optimum temperature, but what's to be their fate after that? They'll need pricking out, which will occupy ten times as much space. Have you room to keep them warm and growing without a check? If so, you're wealthy. The ground will not be warm enough to plant these half-hardies out with profit to them until the end of May at the earliest. Two to three months is a long time to keep them happy without signs of overcrowding or starvation. *(CL)*

Above right: Semper vivum growing on the roof of the Nursery Barn, which is covered with traditional hand made red clay peg tiles. Each tile has two holes in the top, which pegs are pushed through and are in turn used to hook the tile over horizontally fixed wooden battens on the roof.
Right: Gunnera manicata, the water side giant beginning to show the first leaves.

Above: The Edwin Lutyens gate being 'offered up' by the joiner and helped by one of the boys.
Left: Sold in the gift shop, our own labelled natural hemp twine, with a silhouette of Christo's dachshund Dahlia on the wrapper.

15

16

17

18

19

20

21

March

22

23

24

25

26

27

28

Above: The area between the High and Orchard Garden is bordered on four sides by yew hedges, lower by the path and soon to contain the lush summer plants. At this time of year one can see bamboo sticks laid out to define what will be planted where.
Right: The Orchard path to the lower Moat with long grasses and spring flowers.

Left: The terrace dry stone wall full of cracks, perfect for aubretia, and later red valerian, the little Mexican daisy Erigeron karvinskianus and Convolvulus cneorum.
Below: The narrow 4 brick wide path, just enough room for one with a wheel barrow, travels down through blossom to the lower Moat.

29

30

31

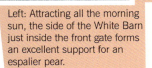

Left: Attracting all the morning sun, the side of the White Barn just inside the front gate forms an excellent support for an espalier pear.

Below: Looking west towards the House, across the flower and vegetable beds. Chestnut posts support the fruit cages, making them quite solid. The ends that are driven into the earth are first charred to prevent them rotting. The structure is covered on every side with galvanised chicken wire, which provides perfect protection from the hungry Dixter bird population.

April

*D*efinitely not summer yet. But the swallows are back. House martins count as swallows for the purposes of seeing the first (which I never seem to anyway). 12 April is cuckoo day, in Sussex (don't ask me why), but cuckoos, the loud monotony of whose persistent call we used to swear at, are now so rare that it is sometimes May before I hear my first. Still, the dawn chorus is terrific and the fact of its being so loud at Dixter is a pleasant reminder of the fact that our sort of garden provides a great many suitable habitats for nesting birds. (CL)

April

1

2

3

4

5

6

7

Above: The entrance Porch to the 15th century Great Hall House, with Lutyens' new extension to the left. The joins in the roof's thousands of clay peg-hung tiles appear seamless. The entrance is dressed on either side with a collection of terracotta pots full of lively groups of spring narcissus, daffodils, hyacinths and auriculas, guarded to the left and right by large box topiary shapes.
Below: A selection of tulip and daffodil leaves with flowers, laid out for teaching purposes by Fergus Garrett.

Previous page: Great Dixter viewed from the south west, showing the Great 15th century Hall House, the Lutyens extension and, on the right, the small hall house originally found nearby in Benenden and bought for £75.

The Edwin Lutyens steps leading to his arch and entrance to the Walled Garden. A mix of pots with shapely plantings against an espalier pear compliment the climb.

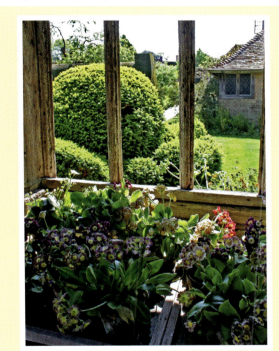

Looking east through the unglazed Gothic-style windows towards the Larder, with a charming arrangement of auricula on the Porch table.

A perfect pair of yew topiary 'coffee pots', close to the curving high hedges of the olive-green Quercus ilex, commonly called holm oak.

Christo's Seasonal Gardening Advice

Daffodils: It is (or should be, unless the season is ridiculously early) the month of the daffodil. I always reckon that 12 April is a date one should be able to rely on for a good display, in our daffodil orchard - some are earlier, some later. First to flower is Narcissus 'Princeps'- marketed to us as 'Princeps Maximus', to make it sound more important. It is like a glorified, tetraploid Lent lily. Next comes the mainstream 'Emperor' a yellow trumpet and always reliable for a fortnight's display but no longer. I do not grow many daffodils in the borders, because the foliage becomes really unsightly, there. (CL)

April

Above: The domestic quarters at the east end of Lutyens' extension to the House. The window in the roof is in the Day Nursery on the first floor.
Above left: The Ticket Office where you are greeted on arrival.

Above: Lutyens' famous circular steps leading to the Orchard and down to the Lower Moat. A bright pattern of blue Myosotis forget-me-nots and tulips frames the view.
Below: A profusion of tulips bringing early colour to the garden.

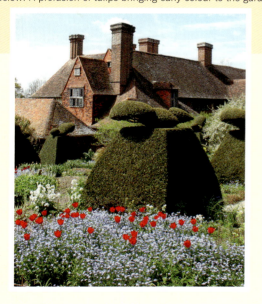

8

9

10

11

12

13

14

15

16

17

18

19

20

21

Above: An espalier Comice pear planted in 1915 against the external chimney at the west end of the original House.
Right: The door to the Nursery Long Barn, where swallows have nested for several centuries, flying in and out to feed their chicks at great speed and with amazing accuracy.

The High Garden vegetable area growing food for the House, visitors and for purchase in the Porch.

Christo's Seasonal Gardening Advice

Pots: The April display is especially lively, our main shop window being either side of the entrance Porch, but we also assemble pots for display in other parts of the garden. Hyacinths look and smell wonderful when gathered together in large pots and I buy at least twenty-five of each variety at a time. They do more than one year, but are eventually planted out. Of the late kinds, one of the most successful is the old double red 'Hollyhock' – a compact cultivar which needs no staking. (Others may need it but probably won't get it.) 'King Cobra' is an intriguing late-flowerer; deep blue but with green tips to its petals. It lurches about, rather, but is endearing, like some friends who have a weakness for the bottle, but always remain charming under the influence. (CL)

April

22

23

24

25

26

27

28

The Sunk Garden with Nathaniel Lloyd's octagonal pool created in 1923. Two opposite sides are longer than the other six, which makes it look relaxed. This garden is surrounded by flagstone paving, then dry stone walling up to grass slopes, and so to the garden's main level, the enclosing framework being barns on two sides, a Lutyens wall on the third and a yew hedge on the fourth. A suntrap indeed.

A rich combination of tulip colours.

Above: Small-cupped Narcissus 'Aflame' planted in amongst the fuchsia.
Right: Dixter's eight Romney sheep enjoying some rich grass next to the car park. Romney sheep are traditional to East Sussex and the marshes.
Below: On the path below the Peacock Topiary, just through the topiary arch is an intriguing area planted out with shrubs and annuals.

Christo's Seasonal Gardening Advice

There is a lot of planting and moving to get on with in the garden. If you don't leave things out of the ground for any length of time, plants can go on being moved right into summer, naturally we keep a hose handy. Do you realize how generous watering needs to be in order to be effective? It does not mean just sprinkling from a hose as you pass. To be thorough and to reach down to the shrub's lowest roots, a watering may need to be continuous for a couple of hours. Naturally, to leave the water on overnight is a wicked waste. Good gardening needs thought and concentration, not just lurching from one extreme to the opposite. (CL)

May

Temperatures are all over the place, in May, but one of the moments that I'm strongly aware of is when, near noon, I'm beneath newly leafed trees, the sun is standing really high and the shadows are short. The sharpness of spring will be present for a long time, but the closeness to summer suddenly makes itself apparent. (CL)

May

1

2

3

4

5

6

7

Top: At the back of the White Barn, this small leadlight window is surrounded by the lush green leaves of a well trained ficus carica 'Brunswick'. This side of the barn borders the Sunk Garden.
Above: Tulipa 'Ballerina'.
Right top: An oriental poppy about to burst.
Right below: Iris reticulata in the Barn Garden.
Below: Tulips are grown as a trial to see which perform best and also serve as cut flowers for the house.

Previous page: The main drive to the House, Garden and Nurseries in early Spring.

Spectacular combination of late flowering tulips

Christo's Seasonal Gardening Advice

Tulips: I will here give my concentrated attention to this favourite flower (favourite with Fergus just as much as with me) in its garden roles, although it continues through much of May, so I shall have to return to it. Bedded out sweet williams can make a terrific early summer display, but you'll want to pep them up in spring – with tulips, of course. The tulips will not need to be lifted until the lupins or sweet williams have themselves completed their display, so the bulbs will have dried off and will be ready to harvest anyway. Just lay them out on racks in a cool, airy shed and they will automatically withdraw their reserves from their leaves back into the bulbs. When the foliage is quite sere, we harvest the bulbs (rubbing off any dirt). All are hung up safe from mice, in open mesh bags. *(CL)*

The east side of the House seen from the Orchard and Meadow. The Meadow, diverse and highly ornamental in itself, is also a valuable natural habitat. The Common Spotted orchid in the foreground.

May

15

16

17

18

19

20

21

Above: Plants along the original back drive above the dry stone wall looking east over the Peacock Topiary.

The open bloom of tulipa 'Bleeding Heart' revealing a magnificent marked and coloured centre.

Right: The strikingly large fennel Ferula communis on the terrace. Growing to a full 8ft tall, with elegant filigree foliage and yellow umbels.

The Malus hupehensis trees in the car park area of the garden love the full sun they receive.

Christo's Seasonal Gardening Advice

If you don't stake and you don't stake in time, plants will collapse and never look the same again. Far more staking is practised in a mixed border than you would ever suspect – if it is well done and invisible. The staking agents are peasticks, alias brushwood, or bamboo canes. So at Dixter we do our sticking on a piecemeal basis and over a period. Use plenty of peasticks: don't be stingy with them so that parts of the plant escape and fall outwards. (CL)

Long grass habitats are an important part of the Great Dixter Estate. Our aim for the future is not only to maintain but also to maximise diversity of plant species, and the insects and birds that rely or flourish on them. In particular, we want to encourage orchids: the Common Spotted orchid (Dactylorhiza fuchsii), twayblade (Listera ovata), Early-Purple (Orchis mascula) and Green-Winged (Orchis morio) orchids.

May

22

23

24

25

26

27

28

Above: Lily-flowered Tulipa 'Ballerina' with Euphorbia x martinii.
Below: The long flagstone path through the Spring Meadow Garden full with camassias flowers, leads to the main door of the house. Great Dixter has no exterior lights except for the small Lutyens lamp adjacent to the front door, so beware if you stay too late.

Christo's Seasonal Gardening Advice

Gourds are extremely easy. Start under glass. 2 seeds to a 3½" pot in a cold frame in early May. In early June harden the seedlings off and plant out. Or push the seeds straight into the ground or into a firm moist part in your compost or manure heap. They like full sun in order to set and ripen the fruit properly. *(CL)*

Above: The Exotic Garden today, bordered on all sides by Yew hedges, offering protection from all winds and thus affording a micro-climate of warmth and protection.
Below: A generous combination of pink gladiolus, blue cranesbill, Verbascum olympicum, salvias, euphorbia, daisies, iris and geraniums.

29

30

31

June

The trouble with June is the speed with which it flashes by. Everything is coming to maturity, but is still young and fresh. There is little dead-heading to worry about, unless you are a rose-grower. The meadows reach a peak, in respect of their wild flower content. The horse pond scintillates. The borders are full of zest; there is much green in them still, but also a great deal of colour from early summer perennials. *(CL)*

June

1

2

3

4

5

6

7

Above: Looking west along the hedge towards the house, with alliums in abundance.

Previous page: A profusion of colourful herbaceous plants.

Above: The clematis 'Marcel Moser'. Blessed by being a Viticella this isn't likely to be attacked by wilt. And is trained to climb up a pillar of the Hovel.
Below: Fergus Garrett in the Sunk Garden.

Above: Rosa macrantha 'Raubritter' rose.
Below: The Papaver orientale 'Karine'

June

Rhododendron 'Sappho' in the garden beyond the Horse Pond.

Above: Grown from seed, the lupin 'The Page' polyhyllus, seen here in the Long Border.
Left: Detail of Lutyens curved wall by the Solar Garden.
Below: The lawns either side of the path leading to the Porch are full of camassias looking regal amongst the grasses, behind them the castle-shaped yew hedge forming the entrance to the Sunk Garden.

8

9

10

11

12

13

14

15

16

17

18

19

20

21

Above: Elegant mixed foxgloves, including 'Sutton's Pink'.
Below: Looking at the house across the Long Border.

Christo's Seasonal Gardening Advice

Lupins quickly become unsightly passengers if included in mixed borders having a later climax, but I love them too much to exclude them altogether. A garden the size of ours should have room for lupins. So I concentrate them here, but throw them out the moment their season is past. There is a large and prolific aphid of lupins, both herbaceous and shrubby, that has reached us from America and become a pest in some years. It is protected by a thick wax coating and we have to spray two or three times to clear it. That is a bore, but it does not happen all the time or on all the lupins. (CL)

June
22

23

24

25

26

27

28

Right: Produce for sale in the Porch, home grown in the fruit and vegetable gardens. Below: The Oast Houses against a dramatic sky.

Right: The White Barn dates from the early 18th century. Part of it once stabled the farm's horses. There was a loft space above for the storage of hay, under a roof that was originally thatched. The section with the big double doors was a coach house in 1910, and Nathaniel Lloyd, already an owner of a motorcar, used it as a garage. It also housed an engine and generator which provided electric lighting for the house.

Christo's Seasonal Gardening Advice

The flexibility of bedding is what makes it exciting. It appeals to the showman element, the delight in a touch of panache that should be in each of us (but, alas is often not). Bedding schemes can be formal. Or bedding can be informal, with plants integrated into the mixed border, which is the type of bedding that is fun and really suits our temperament and needs at Dixter. We sometimes bed out three times in a year in the same space.(CL)

The High Garden, a fantasy playground for Oliver and Selwyn Lloyd.

29

30

A dazzling arrangement of hostas, lupins, ferns, sedums, Californian poppies, in terracotta pots, set out on the Dachshund mosaic flooring of the Solar Garden.

This is the warmest month. At last, the evenings and nights have ceased to be chilly and it is right for picnics at Glyndebourne opera, which is less than an hour's run from Dixter. It is also right for taking our evening drinks to the top of the long border. About seven of us can fit on to Lutyens' seat. It has two return bits at the ends and the one nearest the orchard gives you the best view of the long border itself, but in the gloaming it is just as good to be looking towards the sunset sky, against which the ash tress are silhouetted. *(CL)*

July

1

2

3

4

5

6

7

Above: The Solar courtyard with a well proportioned pot display. Smaller plants in the front, increasingly gaining height to the back of the arrangement.
Right: The delightful Aquilegia 'Kansas'.
Below: The paved sitting-out terrace with just wide enough gaps in the flagstones to provide a playground for self-sowers. Notably Verbena bonariensis with light purple flower heads, but more surprisingly Campanula lactiflora, blown in from a bed some 30m distance, and Dierama pulcherrimum.

Christo's Seasonal Gardening Advice

Fergus and I frequently make a practice of meeting in the garden, early. We are still doing a great deal of planting, in July, for it must be remembered that our aim is to keep the interest going for another three months. With the garden empty, we can do things near to paths without getting in anyone's way. And most importantly we can think – I mean, think creatively on how to carry on with the show. Fergus makes a list of what's available for planting from the frameyard and we work out what to replace the June-flowerers with. There is always something going over that needs attention. *(CL)*

Previous page: A brilliant display of Cosmo bipinnatus 'Dazzler' an excellent magenta. Contrasted with Zinnia 'Chippendale', hollyhocks, daisies and the spectacular Verbascum olympicum.

Above: In the Long Border Ammi majus bishop's flowers with blue larkspur.
Left: The original Royal Sussex trug, crafted entirely by hand in East Sussex, from the sustainable wood of sweet chestnut and willow, Salix Caerulea. Lightweight and strong, in more than seven sizes equivalent to Imperial weights. Sold in our Gift Shop.

Canterbury bells growing by the Oast House wall in the Sunk Garden.

8

9

10

11

12

13

14

July

15

16

17

18

19

20

21

The Horse Pond is so called because the farm horses used to be led into it to drink and wallow at the end of their working day. On the bank a combination of Gunnera manicata, iris and the bamboo Thamnocalamus Tessellatus. In the water waterlily Nymphaea 'Rose Arey' with Orontium aquaticum 'Golden Club' and Water violet Hottonia palustris.

Christo's Seasonal Gardening Advice

The Clematis rows in the Nursery. There are some 230 species and it is not generally realized what a great variety of differing positions are suitable for clematis of one sort or another. A place on a wall may be wired and given over wholly to a clematis or, even better perhaps, it can be allowed to grow over or through another wall shrub of equal or greater vigour. Clematis associate particularly well with roses, whether on walls, pergolas, poles, trellises, tripods or as free growing bushes. In mixed borders and shrubberies, clematis should be included to ramble among any of the more vigorous shrubs. *(CL)*

Above right: The old water butt on wheels, part of Dixter's collection of vintage tools and garden machinery, some of which are on display in the Oast House.

Above: The Lloyd boys with Letitia, complete with a wooden toy yacht with linen sails, ready for action. Christo stands in the front.

A contrasting pot display by the Porch, with daisies, hostas and purple delphiniums.

July

22

23

24

25

26

27

28

Above: The flower of Inula magnifica attracting a stunning 'Peacock' butterfly Inachis io, part of the Nymphalidae family, its wingspan varies between 63mm and 75mm.

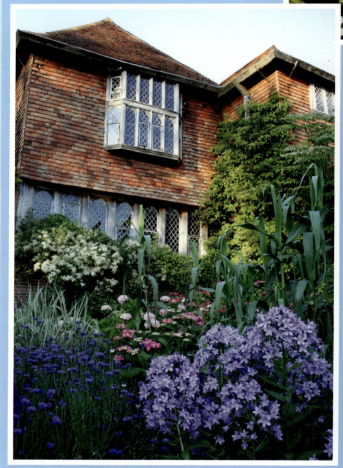

The bay window of the Solar with the office below, hydrangeas, cornflowers and the blue of Campanula lactiflora in the beds in front.

Christo's Seasonal Gardening Advice

It is sensible to grow the plants that like you (and to disdain those that don't). Those raised peat beds that are created by rhododendron – and other calcifuge-plant-lovers forced to garden on alkaline soil are always pathetic. On a one-of-each basis, so as to be able to include as many varieties as possible, they are hopelessly spotty and never make a unified impression. But if you grow the plants that naturally enjoy your company, it is very different. (CL)

Above: Ammi visnage mixed with blue larkspur.
Left: Traditional Hawes watering cans.
Right: The opium poppy Papaver somniferum growing to a height of 1.2m and spread of 30cm.

29

30

31

The view south over the meadow, with one majestic Poplar tree.

August

Fergus and I revel in this season and the many opportunities that it provides. We have been planning for it right through the year and we continue to plan and prepare for September and October. True, the lawns are likely to be brown. They do not come high on our list of priorities and a spot of rain will soon bring them around. In any case, they are neither numerous nor extensive. One has made room for the mosaic, while in the Topiary Garden we now have meadow areas for half the year, instead of lawn. *(CL)*

August

1

2

3

4

5

6

7

Outside the Porch, the pot display of plants creates a colourful welcome to the House.

Previous page: The Zinnia trial in the High Garden.
Inset: Student gardeners on the Terrace under instruction from Fergus.

The Crataegus (hawthorn) tree, just to the right of the steps that bisect the Long Border.

The hot orange of Lilium lancifolium var. fortunei.

Christo's Seasonal Gardening Advice

It is a sound rule to pot off no more rooted cuttings after the end of August. The only exceptions are those plants which can continue to grow at low temperatures throughout the winter. Those that stand still will be more harmed than helped by disturbing them when they cannot make good use of their extra space and new potting soil. That this should be so is a great convenience. It means that your rooted cuttings can be overwintered 10, 12, 14, to a 3½-inch pot, the pot they were struck in, and this is extremely economical of space. By April they can wait no longer. Space must be found, but cold glass protection enough by then. *(CL)*

Ilex Altaclerensis 'Golden King', with bright green leaves and broad yellow margins, bears berries and is therefore female. We use secateurs to give this large holly its annual trim. It was described by Christo as "an almost prickle-free holly that is wonderfully luminous."

August

Above: Marigold 'Strike Marvel'.
Left: Adding shape and contrast in the Exotic Garden, the leaves of Farfugium japonicum grow up to 15cm across.

Right: Creating a bold foliage feature in the Exotic Garden, Colocasia esculenta (elephant's ears) with the familiar dart-shaped leaves of the Taro.
Below: View into the Exotic Garden from the Hovel, the original 14th century cow sheds.

8

9

10

11

12

13

14

15

16

17

18

19

20

21

Above: Looking across the Topiary Lawn to the Hovel as Christo's dachshund, Canna, proceeds in a stately manner towards the Nursery.
Right: The Gatekeeper butterfly Pyronia tithonus, with wingspan from 40mm to 47mm landing on Verbena bonariensis.

The stylish Canna 'General Eisenhower' underway in the Exotic Garden, produce plenty of lush foliage around them so will blend in perfectly. They are best sited at a border's margin, where their entire height can be savoured.

August

22

23

24

25

26

27

28

Above: Cosmos physii seen here with the stripy-leaved cannas are quite something, especially with sunlight behind them. Most self-proclaiming is 'Phasion' also known as 'Durban' and 'Tropicanna'. Right: Zinnia 'Red Flame', you want to be a bit careful not to overfeed it, otherwise it may run to leaf at the expense of the flowers. Both canna and dahlias go well with it too.

The vegetable beds in the High Garden are of a common design used in Edwardian times, where it was an ornamental part of the kitchen garden. Narrow flower borders lined the sides of the paths and behind them were espalier cordon fruit.

Christo's Seasonal Gardening Advice

The last attitude you should take is to think the show is over when you come back from an August holiday. If you live in a frost hollow and expect to get clobbered before September is out, I can only say, rather unsympathetically, that as a gardener you should have thought of that before you decided on where to settle. At last we make a start on cutting and composting the meadow. Not all at once, by any means. Some wait till next month, and by the Horse Pond there is a very worthwhile late display of lesser knapweed, Centaurea nigra. It is a full and busy month but never less than enjoyable. A hint of autumn creeps in from time to time one can be sure of that, but it is no cause for lament. I love autumn. *(CL)*

The jungle-like foliage, hardly leaving a path through the Exotic Garden.

29

30

Above: Table grapes outside the window of the gardener's 'mess' in the Sunk Garden. Below: Oliver Lloyd picking red gages. Preserving, bottling and jam making called for the assistance of all available hands, under the management of Daisy. And Christo called his mother 'the management'.

Ensette ventricosum maurelii. This Ethopian banana native of tropical Africa, has huge olive-green leaves up to 3.6m, but it does require winter protection in a warm greenhouse.

Left: Water pans in the vegetable garden.

September

The danger in a September garden – you see it everywhere – is sleaze. That is what we least want and we keep going through the borders tidying up. They will not look too tidy, as most plants have grown into each other and that looks as relaxed as it is. But ugly remains need constant removal. It makes all the difference. *(CL)*

September

Top: The House and Oast House from the south with smoke trees Rhus continuously flowering in profusion in the Topiary Lawn.
Above: Vegetable Garden showing the planks used by the gardeners to work from, preventing the ground from becoming compressed.

Previous page: The Long Border, 75ft long and 15ft deep (22.8m and 4.5m), one of the longest in England is still full of colour. A mix of trees, shrubs, annuals and perennials, including the beautifully shaped waterlily dahlia 'Pearl of Heemstede', Crocosmia 'Malahide Castle Red' and Salvias 'Superba' with 'Indigo Spires'.

The Gift Shop just beyond the Nursery is housed in the ground floor of one of the estate cottages.

The new Café Loggia, situated by the Gift Shop, is traditionally constructed using oak with clay roof tiles. Created to compliment the style of Great Dixter, it serves beverages and snacks.

1

2

3

4

5

6

7

September

8

9

10

11

12

13

14

Above: Mulberries, with their sharp and sweet fruits, make a handsome head of lacy branches. Our remaining tree suffered badly in the 1987 storm, but now recovered it may make it to 150 years old at the outside.
Right: The characteristic forms of the well trimmed yew shapes on the Topiary Lawn looking toward the Hovel.

Above: Bright pink dahlia 'Fascination'.
Right: The Lutyens designed hand wrought foot scraper.

A view over the Peacock Topiary from the Day Nursery window.

Letitia and Christo Lloyd take tea in the garden.

Christo's Seasonal Gardening Advice

Grass cutting also continues non-stop – I mean the cutting of long grass. Fergus thoroughly enjoys this, as it entails team work - someone on the machine or machines, others loading the grass on the tractor trailer and then building up the compost heap. We like to get the grass on this in as damp a condition as possible, otherwise you end up with an unyielding haystack, instead of nicely rotted compost. To this end we include, as the stack is being built, alternate layers of lime and sulphate of ammonia, and we sprinkle the stack, from overhead, with such water as we can muster. It streams in a satisfying manner and sinks – the faster the better. *(CL)*

15

16

17

18

19

20

21

September

22

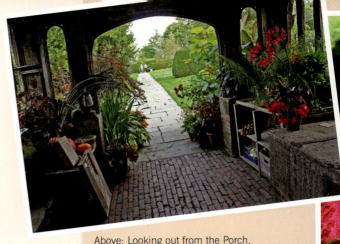

Above: Looking out from the Porch.
Below: Cosmos and Japanese anemone x hybrida 'September Charm' with a running habit that needs checking periodically.

23

24

25

26

27

28

Christo's Seasonal Gardening Advice

On the red dahlia, the medium semi-cactus 'Witteman's Superba' is a special favourite with Fergus and myself; the hint of purple on the reverse side of its rays being especially subtle. I may say that we chose most of those we grow on the trial ground at Wisley. Try and visit this after they have stopped disbudding, say in late September or early October, as you then get a better idea of their performance as garden plants. Disbudding for choice blooms is an artificial practice which is fun in its way, but does not give the results that most of us are looking for. *(CL)*

Above: A late sowing of coleus 'May' is potted individually and brought on under cold glass at Dixter. Leaf patterns and colourings vary a lot but Fergus sorts them into groups when planting out in late July. They are still at their best in September – a Joseph's coat of tapestry colour.

Below: The Asian rice-paper plant Tetrapanax papyriferus (pictured right) in the Exotic Garden, turns us weak at the knees with its large indented palmate leaves. Young Leaves covered with a thick fawn felt are particularly attractive. We lift it in the autumn but the roots left behind start a new colony the following year. The height of this shrub varies according to whether it brings its old wood through the winter or not.

October

Very much a favourite month, this. Even writing a capital O at the start of its name is a pleasure. Of course, the weather can be foul; when can't it? It gave us the great 1987 storm. But October does give us spells of the most delectable weather, too, and the golden warmth of its light invests everything with its glow. Nights have a nip in them but by day the air is soft again and we just need to relax in appreciation. *(CL)*

October

1

2

3

4

5

6

7

Above: The east side of the house seen through the plants of the Orchard Garden.
Right: One of the gardeners cutting the hedges in earlier days, using a device to ensure they are straight.
Below: Topiary peacocks behind a veil of Calamagrostis x acutiflora 'Karl Foerster', the feathery reed grass.

Christo's Seasonal Gardening Advice

The shaggy yew hedges are being assiduously trimmed throughout the month. We start with the peacocks, so that they shall look smart at the time when the double hedges of Aster lateriflorus 'Horizontalis' are building up their flower power. Then we move to the long border and the stretch of hedge running at right angles from that down the side of the orchards. Next, across the orchard to the exotic garden, but here we trim only their outside and top; the inside is left till we have cleared the beds in front of them. On, across to the Topiary Garden and here we first of all cut the long grass, so formality is at last restored to this area which I have of recent years allowed to take its ease during the summer months. (CL)

Previous page: The Horse Pond in autumn takes on an air of reflective tranquility, with swamp Cypress Taxodium distichum on the right, one of the few deciduous conifers growing in Britain.

Above: An early picture of topiary in the Peacock Garden being shaped by a gardener.
Below: One of today's gardeners combing the hedges between cuts, which helps get rid of unwanted trimmings.

Below: Nerine bowdenii is a splendid autumn performer and is as vivid a pink (with a dash of mauve) as you could imagine and an entirely un-autumn colour, but no less welcome for that. Here strikingly combined with the leaves of Prunus glandulosa 'Alba Plena', the flowering almond, in the Sunk Garden looking towards the Solar.

8

9

10

11

12

13

14

October

Top: The colour of the six House chimneys complimented by grasses, many still in perfect shape going into winter, contrast well with the cream of Anaphalis 'Yedoensis'.
Above: The path leading through the Orchard Garden is lined on both sides by Buxus sempervirens.

Any fig that needs tying in to a wall should be dealt with by March. They are grown mainly for their leaves as wall decoration, and their pale grey stems also look good in winter. To fruit well, as little pruning as possible should be practised, as they fruit from the tips of their previous year's young shoots.

Plants in the Exotic Garden wrapped for winter with straw and old sacking to protect them from frost. Tree ferns and bananas receive the same treatment and are wrapped to the level at which they will start growing the following year.

The Kitchen yard, designed by Lutyens to provide room for boot-cleaning, coal and fuel storage. The yard was also used as a pig sty.

Christo's Seasonal Gardening Advice

Many grasses are in perfect shape, now, and it always amazes me how many of them choose to flower in autumn. Although my garden is largish, it is divided into compartments and I think that most of these grasses show up best as solo features rather than in groups. They have quite sufficient structure and presence to deserve to stand well above the surrounding plants. This may often be achieved by sitting them on a promontory or in a corner, but fairly near to a border's margin. Two of my most effective are 'Windspiel' and 'Transparent', both of which come under Molinia caerulea subsp. Arundinacea. *(CL)*

15

16

17

18

19

20

21

October

22

23

24

25

26

27

28

Above: Hops being loaded into the Oast Houses, circa 1920. The three distinctive conical shape chimneys are finished with cowls on the top controlling the airflow, ensuring a good draught was maintained to keep the fires going, which then dried the hops spread out over the first floor of the building. The hot air from the furnace was then drawn out through the cowls.
Right: The window of the Solar viewed from the Barn Garden.

Christo's Seasonal Gardening Advice

The sharp smell of October is most attractive and is largely created, I imagine, by drifts of fallen leaves. I never tire of scuffling through them. Unless the leaves are seriously shading plants that need to see the light, we are in no hurry to pick them up and take them, as we eventually do, to spread around rhododendrons as a moisture-retaining mulch. We wait for the winds to blow them into sheltered corners, from where they will the more easily be gathered. Another reason for autumn's smell must surely be the abundance of fruiting fungi. I always hope that there will be worthwhile crops of mushrooms in our meadows. Now that these have been mown, the mushroom caps gleam from a distance. The best chance of a crop is when rains follow drought, but it needs to stay mild, too. Often, rain is followed by cold weather. *(CL)*

29

30

31

Above: Looking north east with the guard-like Peacock topiary.
Left: A winter cabbage.

Above: The fruit and vegetable gardens seen from the very eastern part of the estate.
Inset above right: Our 19th century wheelbarrows are high sided and made mainly out of wood.
Right: Leeks grown in troughs, which are filled in with soil to cover the stems, effectively blanching the vegetables to make them whiter and less tough.

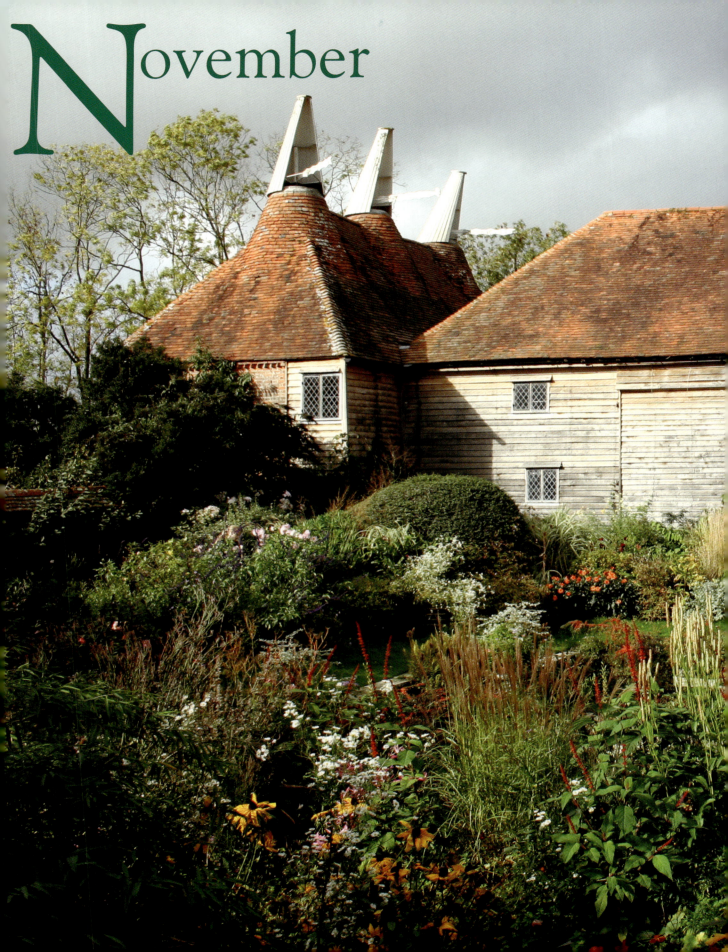

November

*N*ovember can be a month of largely beautiful weather. I remember the one when we were having our huge barn roof re-tiled. The task had had to await our being closed to the public; hence the choice of this unpropitious moment. I took photographs of work in progress and they were invariably backed by blue skies. There wasn't a hitch. Good weather in November is not as rare as you think. Start making daily notes on it and you will see that I am right. *(CL)*

November

1

2

3

4

5

6

7

Top: Samples of wood labelled for identification.
Above: Inside the Great Barn - which now houses the woodcraft workshop. Here traditional skills are being practised, splitting chestnut logs with a 'froe and mallet' to make ladders, and legs for our stools, benches and tables. Just a few of the items now available to purchase at the Gift Shop.

Small sheep hurdles, made on the estate and used for holding plants back from flopping over paths.

Previous page: The Oast House and Great Barn with Himalayacalamus bamboo In the foreground. The barn is 500 years old and one of the largest and most significant surviving medieval timber frame barns in the south-east of Britain. The adjoining 19th century brick built Oast House has feeding troughs, remnants of the original threshing floor and the 18th century grain store is elevated on blocks to discourage rats.

Christo's Seasonal Gardening Advice

I have to admit that the weather, as well as the day length, can be most unco-operative, but Fergus has a system of laying out boards to stand on when planting, so that the planter's weight is distributed and does not hopelessly poach the ground where he has stood. The idea is to clear away the summer bedding and replant all in one swoop, if not in one day. You will find that the ground under the old bedding is always friable and reasonably dry, until the cover is removed. If you can immediately fork it over and plant, conditions will be ideal. But woe betide if you fork over and have no daylight left to do the planting. Sure as fate, it will rain overnight and all those air spaces that have been created will fill with water like a sponge. *(CL)*

Top: The Sunk Garden taking on its winter mantle.
Above: A new compost heap is started every year stacked high with meadow cuttings, waste and spent material. These huge piles take three years to become compost, which is in turn winter dug into the soil. Bumble bees, grass snakes and spiders will all make their home here for the duration.

November

Above: Tender plants are brought into the House for the winter.
Left: The Lutyens gate complete with an estate cat.
Below: The highly ornamental gourds on the window sill of the Solar.

Christo's Seasonal Gardening Advice

Plants can be kept on window sills or in the room, always with danger from draughts. Traditionally, the bathroom is a good place because of its high humidity. Cellars are frost-free and good for storage if the temperature is level and cool. The same proviso applies to a shed or a garage. They can be used for dahlias and cannas stored dormant. Every year there will be unexpected losses, sometimes our own fault, and sometimes through circumstances we could never have planned for. You just have to be stoic about this; learn the lesson and forge on. *(CL)*

8

9

10

11

12

13

14

15

16

17

18

19

20

21

Above: The external chimney which warms the Parlour and the Solar alike.
Below: A self sewn Dipsacus sylvestris (teasel) is weighty enough to act as a skeleton throughout winter.

Christo's Seasonal Gardening Advice

Wet though it is, we must do everything possible now, while the weather remains mild. Once the ground becomes cold as well as wet, one's body and mind quickly grows numb and this is a useless state for a gardener to be in. There will be time enough for the hedge brushing and bonfire making later on. The emphasis now must be on clearing, digging and planting. Clay gardeners must proceed with the greatest circumspection. *(CL)*

November

22

23

24

25

26

27

28

The House was used during the First World War (1914-1918) as a recuperation centre for soldiers returning from the front line. Seen here in the Great Hall, soldiers and nurses during a mealtime.

Above: Inside the Hovel with the splendid wooden table and benches. Above right: Weights are used to keep the lids of the cold frames together in the Nursery when not in use.

Christo's Seasonal Gardening Advice

We dig rough, turning over large clods which frost breaks down, but first we dress the ground liberally with our own compost, most of which was made from grass taken off the meadow areas. Gourds (and cucumbers, long since finished) will have been grown on the old heaps. When their foliage has been wind-blasted, you can the better see what your crop is and it'll not now be too late to collect and use it (for ornament) so long as there's not been a frost. (CL)

Above: Dixter wooden boards are laid on top of the earth to prevent compressing the ground. Small sheep hurdles are used at border edges and corners to prevent people walking on the earth.
Right: Old soil and spent John Innes being mixed in and recycled for another job.
Below: A view of the 15th century Hall with the north window of the Solar.

29

30

December could be as dreary a month as January, but the festive season prevents this and provides a much-needed break. Even the weeds understand the rules; their growth has almost come to a standstill. But the forward pulse of the year is evident from week to week, if not from day to day. The much-loved garden, all that's new in it and all that's old, is barely marking time and we are ready to steer it forward into another year. *(CL)*

December

Above: The long entrance path up to the Porch.
Left: The House seen from over the frozen Horse Pond.
Below: The long ancient roof of the Hovel, red clay tiles and oak timbers holding up well against the rigours of winter.

Previous page: The House, Horse Pond and Peacock Garden viewed from the drive after a snowfall in early December.

1

2

3

4

5

6

7

8

9

10

11

Above: The 'coffee pot' topiary with the big chimney.
Below: The Nursery Barn thick with snow but always open for business right through the year.

12

13

14

Christo's Seasonal Gardening Advice

I refer to early December as the phony winter, as the season seldom shows its teeth till later on. In fact, there are often a whole lot of reminders of summer flowers, which can be included in bunches to bring indoors. We shall still be desperately catching up, in these early weeks, with many tulip bulbs to find places for. The last of them get lined out in a spare plot. These are usually the smallest, for growing on to use in the borders a year later, but some are of flowering size and come in for handy picking, to include in mixed borders. *(CL)*

December
15

16

17

18

19

20

21

Above: The old Dixter bike leaning up against the door of the Friends' information room.
Left: The original power and voltage units now exhibited for visitors' inspection.

Right: The old horse stables in a space to the right of the main pair of doors in the White Barn. Constructed of wood and divided down the centre to create two spaces, the floor is constructed of cobbles and brick.

Above: The distinctive wavy lines of the pennants on the cowls of the Oast House chimneys.
Below: The Great Barn and Oast House newly restored with stairs up to the hop drying floor.

December

22

23

24

25 Christmas Day

26 Boxing Day

27

28

Right: A covered area on the back of the Great Barn, with various stools and mini sheep hurdles made in our wood work shop. Facing east it is a good place to sit and admire the Sunk garden.
Below: A selection of old tools in the shop, which make perfect Christmas presents

Above: Every year the main door is dressed with a seasonal wreath using foliage from the garden in readiness for the Christmas Fair and the coming festivities.

Christo's Seasonal Gardening Advice

Whatever happens after me, I should like to record my hope that no one, for lack of personal creativity, will fall back on the old cliché of recreating this, that or the other with the same plants that Christopher Lloyd used and in the same way.
We have too many fossilized gardeners in the world, but they do exist and I should like to think of one or other of them having a good time at Dixter for many years to come. (CL)

29

30

New Years Eve 31

The Topiary Lawn after heavy snowfall, circa 1956, photographed by Col Evans, who lived next door.

Above centre: Aaron Bertelsen working in the vegetable area of the High Garden

GREAT DIXTER RECIPES

The garden produce played a supporting role in Christopher Lloyd's culinary skills, which were constantly exercised for the benefit of his wide circle of friends. Great Dixter and its people have become a magnet, drawing professional gardeners, students of gardening and the public from around the world.

Here are two of Christo's recipes for you to enjoy.

GREAT DIXTER CHUTNEY

½ oz powdered ginger
4 lb apples
6 lb ripe tomatoes
1 teaspoon cayenne pepper
4 lb brown sugar shallots
1 lb sultanas
4 oz finely chopped onions
2 oz salt
2 pints of malt vinegar

Peel, core and slice the apples, and then weigh them. Cook these first separately.

Skin the tomatoes by dipping them in hot water, and chop them roughly. Put all the ingredients in a preserving pan and boil for 1 hour or more until the mixture thickens.

Store in broad-mouthed jars in a cool place.

CHRISTO'S ELDERFLOWER CORDIAL

I make my elderflower cordial by putting half a dozen large, recently opened flower heads in a saucepan, together with five lemons, halved and their juice squeezed.

Add 340g / ¾lb of sugar and a gallon of boiling water.

This is left to steep for three days before being strained into bottles.

It is not for long keeping! *(CL)*

Garden plan

Create a plan of your garden to help organise your planting to get the best from it. The grid is to draw out the whole area of your garden, or any individual beds at a larger scale if the planting is more involved.

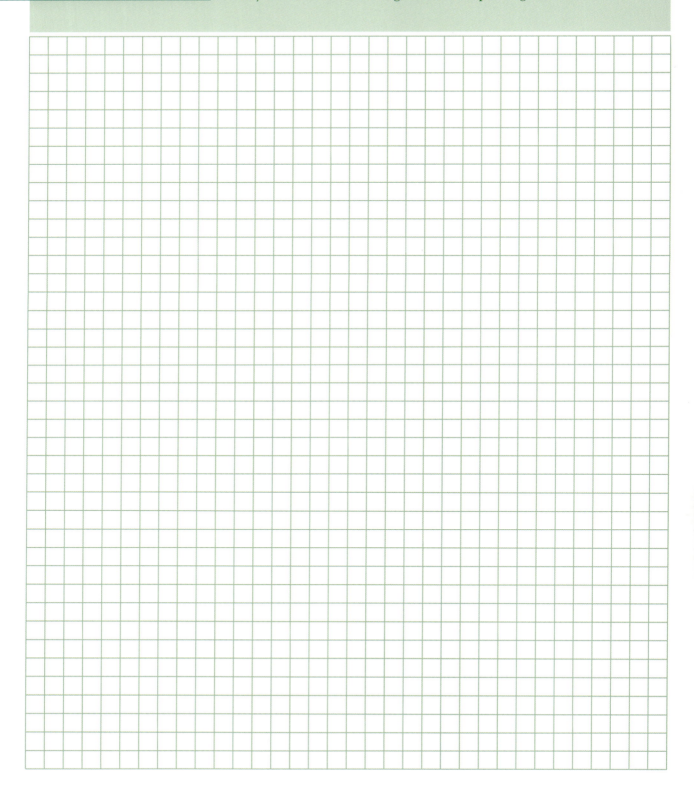

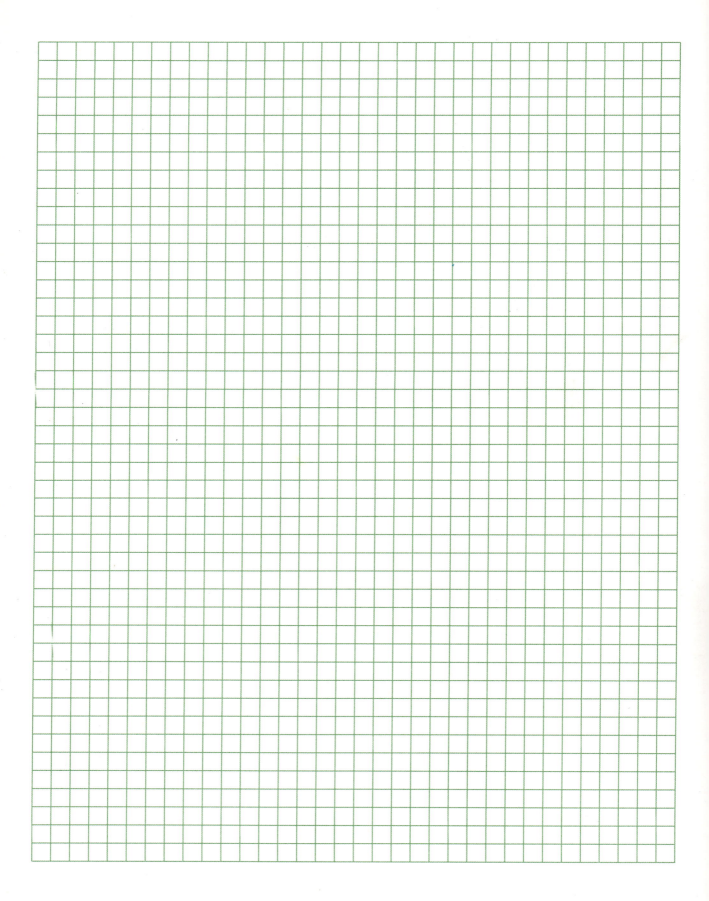